# BE
# BRAVE

BE BRAVE

An Hachette UK Company
www.hachette.co.uk

Vie Books, an imprint of Summersdale Publishers Ltd
Part of Octopus Publishing Group Limited
Carmelite House
50 Victoria Embankment
LONDON
EC4Y 0DZ
UK

www.summersdale.com

Printed and bound in China

ISBN: 978-1-78783-699-0

Substantial discounts on bulk quantities of Summersdale books are available to corporations, professional associations and other organizations. For details contact general enquiries: telephone: +44 (0) 1243 771107 or email: enquiries@summersdale.com.

# BE BRAVE

## A Child's Guide to Overcoming Shyness

Poppy O'Neill
Foreword by Amanda Ashman-Wymbs

# CONTENTS

# PART 3: IT'S OK TO BE ME

# PART 4: HOW TO BE BRAVE

# PART 5: TAKING GOOD CARE OF YOURSELF.................112

# PART 6: CELEBRATE YOURSELF....................................128

# THE END.................................................................136

# FOREWORD

*Amanda Ashman-Wymbs, Counsellor and Psychotherapist,
registered and accredited by the British Association of
Counselling and Psychotherapy*

Having had the experience of raising a family and working therapeutically with children and young people in the private and public sector for over a decade, it is clear to me that issues around being shy and anxious are widespread, and it is often difficult for children (and their parents) to know how to manage these. It is so important that the child feels respected and valued for being themselves and that any techniques to develop a child's confidence are offered in warm, sensitive and engaging ways.

*Be Brave* by Poppy O'Neill has clearly achieved this. It is a wonderful resource for children and their parents and offers the child easy-to-follow pathways for developing confidence. It is written in age-appropriate, clear language with a friendly monster character called Jem accompanying the child on their journey through many fun activities and games. These help the child to value their own and everyone else's uniqueness, and acknowledge the resources they already have within. The exercises raise awareness of their thoughts and offer techniques on cultivating more helpful ones; they assist the child to understand and communicate their emotions and try out new ways of being brave. There is also an introduction to mindfulness techniques which enable the child to become more self-aware and support a recognition of their connection to the world around them, their senses, and the peace within them – this naturally brings freedom and confidence. The book takes an informative and holistic approach; it covers in friendly ways the value of good nutrition, sleep and exercise alongside offering simple psychological techniques for healthy change.

I highly recommend this valuable and much needed book which truly supports our children to be fully themselves and allows them to learn again to feel comfortable in their bodies and lives.

# INTRODUCTION: A GUIDE FOR PARENTS AND CARERS

*Be Brave* is a practical guide to help children find their inner bravery and overcome shyness. Using activities and ideas based on techniques developed by child psychologists, this book will help your child develop the tools to view their own shyness and bravery in a new light – allowing them to break free of the ways in which shyness holds them back.

We use the word "shy" to describe many behaviours – being an introvert, social anxiety, speaking softly – so it's important to note that there's nothing wrong with those who are labelled "shy". Enjoying time alone and choosing when to use your voice can be really positive traits. However, shyness can also indicate anxiety around social situations, trying new things and being your authentic self.

Perhaps your child is struggling to make friends or seems to fade into the background when around others. Maybe they've been affected by bullying or teasing in the past or they avoid taking risks because the idea of speaking up or failing is too frightening for them. The thing about bravery is, it's not about being fearless – it's about feeling uncomfortable emotions and persevering anyway.

This book is aimed at children aged 7–11, an age when awareness of social relationships increases – meaning they start to care what other people think of them. Coupled with the first signs of puberty and new pressures from school, it's no wonder this can be a time when children shrink or hide themselves in order to fit in. If this sounds like your child, you're not alone. With your support and patience, your child can build their bravery and self-assurance so that they can face challenges, be themselves and grow into a confident, happy and well-balanced young person.

# Signs of shyness in children

Look out for signs such as these, as they may indicate that shyness is holding your child back:

- They are reluctant to try new things

- They are reluctant to join in with activities

- They do not speak up in groups

- They seem to have a very different personality at home, in school and in company

- They describe a solitary future adult life for themselves

- They have difficulty forging friendships

- They are nervous or distressed at the thought of being away from you

- They have been teased or bullied

It can be useful to keep track of your child's shy behaviour in a journal. This can help you get a clear idea of how much your child's life is affected by shyness and can sometimes allow you to "connect the dots" between seemingly unrelated behaviours.

It can be difficult to look at our children's mental and emotional health – sometimes we as parents and carers might identify ways in which our own behaviour has been unhelpful. Be kind to yourself and know that you are giving your child a tremendous gift by taking an interest and supporting them. Bravery cannot be achieved by any quick fix; it is a lifelong habit, which means it's never too late to start developing it.

# How to use this book

••••••••••••••••••••••••••••••••••••••••••••••••••••••••••••••••••••••••••

This book is for your child, so the amount of involvement you have will depend on how much they want or need from you. Some children might be happy working through the activities by themselves, while others might need a little guidance and encouragement.

Even if your child wants to complete the activities alone, it's a good idea to show an interest and start a conversation about the book – anything they've learned or realized, any parts they've found unhelpful or boring. A small way you can help your child to grow their bravery is by calmly listening to their honest feedback about a book you've given them!

The activities are designed to get your child thinking about the way their emotions and minds work, so reassure them there are no wrong answers and they can go at their own pace. Hopefully this book will help you and your child to gain a greater understanding of each other and how shyness and bravery work. However, if you have any serious concerns about your child's mental health, your GP is the best person to go to for further advice.

# HOW TO USE THIS BOOK: A GUIDE FOR CHILDREN

Have you ever been called "shy"? It's a word that's used a lot! Perhaps you didn't want to play with someone, or do something… or sometimes you don't want to speak. All of these things are OK.

Sometimes, though, feelings of shyness can get in the way of being yourself and having fun. Here are some signs that might be happening for you:

 You sometimes don't speak at all because you're too nervous

You feel embarrassed about the way you look or your personality

You feel like you aren't as good at things as others

 You find it hard to speak up for yourself

If that sounds like you, you're not the only one! Lots of children feel this way – they just have different ways of showing it on the outside. This book is here to help you find your voice and act with bravery when it matters, while still being your brilliant self.

There are loads of activities and ideas to help you learn about thoughts, emotions, shyness and bravery. You can go at your own pace, and you can get help from your grown-up at any point. There might be things in the book that you'd like to talk about with your grown-up, too. This book is for you and about you, so there are no wrong answers – you're the expert!

# INTRODUCING
# JEM THE MONSTER

Hi, good to meet you! I'm Jem and I'm here to guide you through this book. Do you ever feel shy? I certainly do… and that's OK. If you feel like your shyness is stopping you from enjoying life, then help is here. There are lots of cool ideas to learn about and fun activities to do. Are you ready? Let's go.

# PART 1: SHYNESS AND ME

In this chapter we're going to learn all about you and all about shyness. Getting to know yourself and how shyness shows up in your life is a really important part of growing into a brave person.

# ACTIVITY: ALL ABOUT ME

First, let's find out all about you!

My name is...

I am

_____

years old

My family is...

My favourite food is...

My ideal weekend would be...

I'm good at...

I'm a good friend when I...

# I AM UNIQUE, JUST LIKE MY FINGERPRINT!

Have you ever noticed the lines on the skin at the tips of your fingers? These are your fingerprints. Look closely, there's a lot to see!

Everyone's fingerprints are unique, and it's the same for personalities! Your personality is made up of all the things you think, feel and do. There is no one in the world quite like you.

Let's get to know your personality a little better.

I like it when...

My favourite thing is...

My talent is...

I don't like it when...

# WHAT DOES IT MEAN TO BE SHY?

Sometimes we feel shy because we prefer spending time alone, in small groups rather than big groups, or with people we know really well, and that's OK.

But other times feeling shy means we are scared to speak or to join in. When we feel this way, it's a kind of anxiety. Anxiety is our brain's way of keeping us safe.

Thousands of years ago, humans lived in caves and there were dangerous animals around that could hurt or kill them, like wolves and sabretooth tigers. So, their brains developed a way of keeping them safe and alive. Whenever a human sensed danger, their brains filled their bodies with an uncomfortable feeling – anxiety. To stop the feeling, humans ran away from the danger.

Human brains have changed in lots of ways since then, but anxiety remains, because it works really well to keep us safe.

Today, we mostly don't need to watch out for wolves or sabretooth tigers, but our brains still look for danger in the same way.

If you find speaking up in social situations nerve-wracking, you're not alone! Your brain is picking up on the danger of things that feel horrible… like being laughed at, being rejected or making a mistake. Your brain is telling you to stay quiet in order to stay safe.

But staying small and quiet out of fear means you miss out on so much of life, and your friends miss out on getting to know the real, brilliant you.

# LOOKING FOR SIGNS

## Signs of shyness

Shyness can show up in different ways. Here are some of them:

- ☀ You want to stay close to your grown-up
- ☀ Busy places make you feel very worried
- ☀ It feels very difficult to speak sometimes
- ☀ Your voice becomes very quiet
- ☀ You feel embarrassed easily

## Signs of bravery

There's a lot of bravery in shyness, too. Here are a few signs that you're brave:

- ☀ You stick with something, even if you feel shy
- ☀ When you feel uncomfortable, you find ways to feel more relaxed
- ☀ You try your best
- ☀ You talk about your feelings
- ☀ You don't do things just because everybody else is doing them

# ACTIVITY: WHAT'S BRAVE FOR ME?

Different people find different things easy or hard. It takes bravery to do hard things. What things are brave for you?

Colour the things that you find really difficult red, the things that are a bit tricky yellow and use green for the things that are easy for you. Add some of your own, if you like!

Speaking up in class

Making a new friend

Trying something new

Using my voice

Looking at someone when I'm talking to them

Eating lunch in the lunch hall

Going to school

Playing sports

Being somewhere busy

Speaking to new adults

Being somewhere loud

Playing with a pet

Speaking up at home

Playing by myself

Reading a book

Going to a friend's house for the first time

Talking to my best friend

Talking to kids who are older than me

Talking to kids who are younger than me

# HOW DOES SHYNESS AFFECT ME?

Shyness affects everyone differently. It can mean feeling embarrassed by parts of your body, your voice or a fact about yourself. It can also mean feeling afraid or unsafe in certain situations, even when there's nothing dangerous happening around you.

Perhaps shyness makes it difficult for you to make friends, or you feel like you have to hide something about yourself when you're with other people.

Perhaps there are particular things that shyness stops you from doing, like going to the swimming pool or speaking on the phone.

Write or draw about it here:

# ACTIVITY: WHAT DOES SHYNESS LOOK LIKE AND FEEL LIKE FOR ME?

How does shyness feel in your body? It might be a small, tight feeling, a heavy or hot one, in your chest, your tummy or shoulders… everyone is different. Draw or write about how shyness feels inside on the body below.

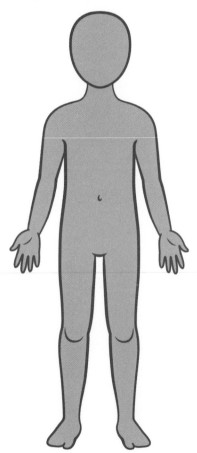

How does your body move or change when you feel shy? How might a friend spot that you are feeling shy? Perhaps you bite your nails, scrunch up your toes or your cheeks turn red. Draw or write about how shyness looks on the outside.

# ACTIVITY: ALL ABOUT ME QUIZ

Take this quiz to get to know more about your personality. Circle the answer that feels the best for you.

1. **When you listen to a song, what do you remember about it most easily?**

   a. The words

   b. The tune

   c. How it made me feel

2. **When you're with friends, what's more important?**

   a. Getting along

   b. Having my opinion heard

   c. Making sure everyone can be themselves

3. **My bedroom is...**

   a. Nice and tidy

   b. Pretty messy

   c. Full of stuff, but everything has its place

**4. When I paint, I prefer...**

a. Instructions to follow

b. To paint whatever I like

c. Some inspiration to get me started

**5. I have...**

a. One best friend

b. Lots of friends

c. A group of close friends

**Mostly A:** You're very observant, which means you notice the details other people miss. Sensitivity is your super power and you feel good when life is simple and straightforward.

**Mostly B:** You're a free spirit and you can't help but be your brilliant self all the time! Bravery is your super power and you feel most comfortable when you can let your imagination run wild.

**Mostly C:** You're a great friend to both yourself and other people. Imagination is your super power and you come up with brilliant ideas. You feel best when everyone is getting along.

# I AM
# BRAVE

# ACTIVITY: IMAGINE YOUR BRAVEST SELF

Close your eyes and imagine: what would your life be like if fear or shyness never held you back? Let your imagination go wild... You can think about yourself now or when you're older. Be as ambitious as you like! Decorate this room for your bravest self – try to include all the things you'd love to do with your life.

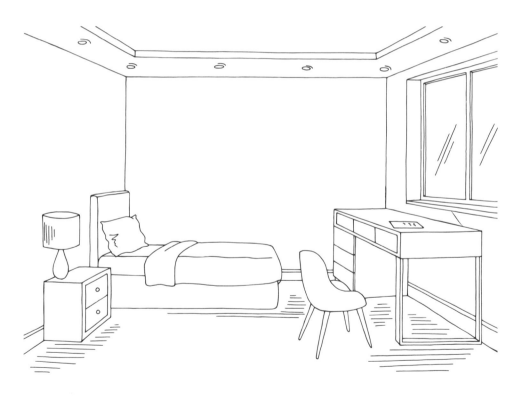

# PART 2: BRAVERY BOOSTERS

In this chapter we'll explore ways you can give yourself extra bravery power!

# WHAT IS MINDFULNESS?

Mindfulness means slowing down and really paying attention to something. You can do almost anything mindfully… from brushing your teeth to walking, and from homework to breathing. When you concentrate on what is happening right at this moment, your mind can have a break from thinking about things that might happen in the future and things that have already happened. It's a bit like a holiday for your brain.

# LISTEN TO YOUR BODY

Let's try a mindful activity called a body scan. Close your eyes and imagine a laser or a beam of light passing over your body. Start at the top of your head – then move your attention laser slowly down past your ears. See how slowly you can move the laser past your shoulders, your tummy, over your legs and to the tips of your toes.

How did that feel? Did you notice any feelings in your body – aches, itches, somewhere that needs to stretch?

Doing a body scan is a great way to calm down if you're feeling worried, scared or having trouble falling asleep.

# ACTIVITY: HOW DO YOU FEEL RIGHT NOW?

Are you feeling an emotion right now? Can you name it? Maybe you're feeling more than one thing or how you feel doesn't have a name. Decorate this heart with how you're feeling right this minute. You can use pictures, colour, patterns, words… whatever you like!

# ACTIVITY: KEEP TRACK OF YOUR MOODS

Pick a different colour for each different mood and use this mood tracker to keep a record of your moods across the space of a week.

|      | Morning | Afternoon | Evening | Night |
|------|---------|-----------|---------|-------|
| Mon  |         |           |         |       |
| Tues |         |           |         |       |
| Wed  |         |           |         |       |
| Thur |         |           |         |       |
| Fri  |         |           |         |       |
| Sat  |         |           |         |       |
| Sun  |         |           |         |       |

○ happy    ○ excited    ○ bored    ○ calm

○ angry    ○ sad    ○ worried    ○ shy

Do you notice any patterns? Perhaps there's a time of day that feels particularly easy or difficult for you. How could you make changes to your day so that the difficult parts feel a bit easier?

# ACTIVITY: 54321 SENSES

Stop everything you're doing and use your fingers to count down…

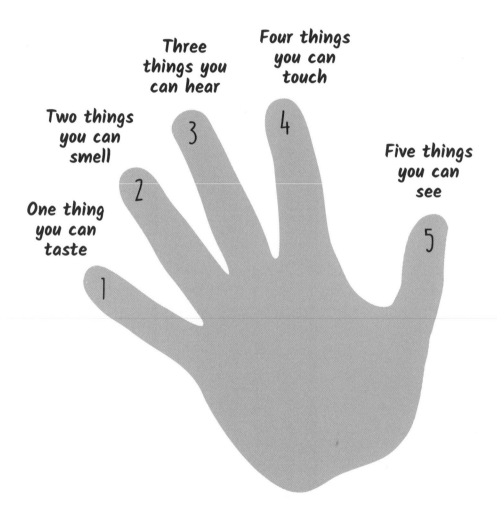

Four things
you can
touch

Three
things you
can hear

Two things
you can
smell

Five things
you can
see

One thing
you can
taste

Jem can see birds, clouds, leaves, a bee and soft green fur

Jem can touch soft fur, grass, tree bark, earth

Jem can hear the wind, cars driving, hands clapping

Jem can smell cut grass, wet mud

Jem can taste apple

This clever trick will help you feel calm wherever you are.

# ACTIVITY: BREATHING SHAPES

When you need to grow some extra bravery, concentrating on your breathing is a great way to do it. Trace your finger slowly around these breathing tracks. Imagine breathing in bravery and breathing out fear.

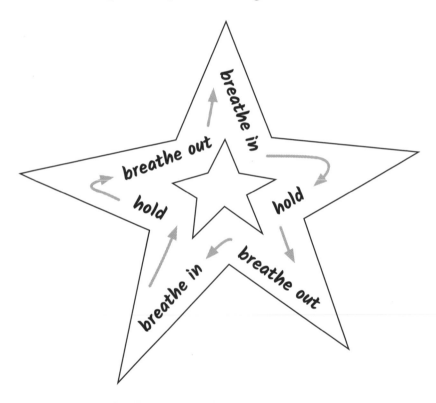

Why not paint a breathing shape onto a smooth pebble or a piece of sturdy card? Keep your breathing track with you, so you can grow bravery wherever you go.

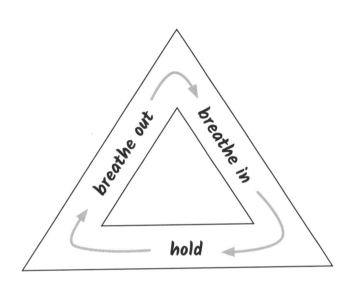

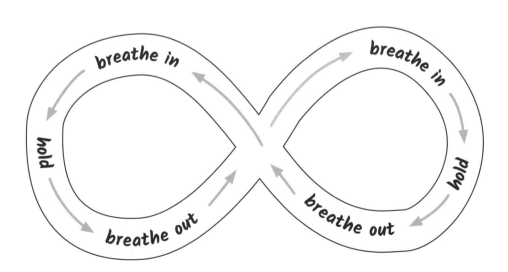

# ACTIVITY: QUICK CALMERS

Did you know that moving your body calms down your mind? It's true! When you're about to do something brave, try one of these activities beforehand to help yourself feel calm and confident:

 Drum a tune on your legs

 Jump on the spot

 Stomp in a circle

 Tap your shoulders

 Swing your arms from side to side

If you feel silly doing these things where someone might see you, do them in your room before you leave the house, or find somewhere quiet and private.

# ACTIVITY: IS YOUR BODY TENSE OR RELAXED?

A good way to check if a feeling of shyness is coming from fear or if it is just you being yourself is to see how relaxed your body is.

Are your shoulders hunched?

Is your breathing quick?

Is your teeth
Are your teeth clenched?

Are you covering up your tummy with your hands?

These are telltale signs that there's a lot of tension in your body and that your mind thinks it needs to keep your body safe from something. Try one of the quick calmers to help your body and mind relax.

# I CAN DO
# HARD THINGS

# WHAT IS SELF-TALK?

Self-talk is how we speak to ourselves in our heads, as well as how we talk *about* ourselves with our voices. It has a big effect on how brave, confident and calm we feel.

Think of a time you felt shy. Can you remember some of the thoughts you had about yourself at the time? If so, write them here:

For example, "I'm welcome here" or "No one wants to talk to me."

_____

_____

That's what self-talk sounds like. How much kindness and patience is there in your self-talk? How would you feel if someone else spoke to you in that way?

Here's some good news: you have the power to choose kinder and more patient self-talk. If you hear yourself using unfriendly words about yourself, you can simply choose kinder words. For example:

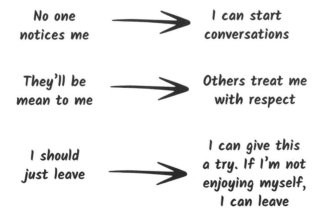

# ACTIVITY: MIX-AND-MATCH POWER WORDS

Choose which words on the right to connect to the words on the left and you'll unlock power words that will help you feel brave.

**I am as...**          **as a...**

strong                  lion

brave                   river

mighty                  mountain

calm                    beaver

curious                 ocean

smart                   dolphin

determined              monkey

special                 tree

| I am as... | as a... |
|---|---|
| powerful | dog |
| playful | ox |
| funny | flower |
| confident | cat |
| kind | owl |
| creative | horse |
| resilient | llama |
| friendly | unicorn |
| beautiful | sloth |
| wise | flamingo |
| happy | shark |

# ACTIVITY: TIME FOR A BREATHER

Reading this book might feel quite frustrating – it's always telling you to be braver and do hard things! On this page we're going to take a break.

You're doing really, really well and you're brilliant exactly as you are. You don't have to change anything about yourself, and you don't have to do difficult things until you're ready.

Can you think of some kind words to tell yourself right now? Here are a few to start you off:

I am doing my best

I am a good person

I am already brave

Now you try:

# ACTIVITY: THREE DIFFERENT STORIES

There are always at least three different ways to think about something that hasn't happened yet.

Is there something coming up that you're feeling nervous about? Perhaps you're thinking of giving up or not taking part.

First, write down the story your fear is telling you:
    For example: I'll lose the competition and feel embarrassed.

_____

Now, write down what your hope is telling you:
    For example: It could be fun and we might even win.

_____

Lastly, write down what you think will probably happen:
    For example: I'll have a nice time with my teammates.

_____

# ACTIVITY: I WAS BRAVE WHEN...

Can you think of a time when you were brave enough to do something that felt really difficult or scary?

_____

_____

Can you remember what helped you find the courage to do that?

_____

_____

How could you use your answer to the last question to help you find bravery today and in the future?

_____

_____

Have you tried the difficult or scary thing again?

_____

_____

If yes, how did it feel the last time?

_____

_____

If no, does it still feel like a difficult or scary thing?

_____

_____

**Thinking about times you were brave in the past is a great way of building bravery for the future.**

# ACTIVITY: MAGIC WORDS

Thoughts can work like magic bravery spells. The trick is to find out which words and thoughts are magic for you. Everyone is unique, so their magic words will be unique, too!

Jem finds these magic words calming:

Try a few of these magic words. Say them to yourself and see if they have a magic calming effect on your body. When you find one that works, write it here:

I am
wise

I am
grateful

I can
take a
break

I am
mighty

I am
peaceful

I see my
strengths

I can
choose my
thoughts

I have
an epic
personality

I am
brave

I am
strong

I am
thoughtful

I am
magical

I am
safe

I love
me

# ACTIVITY: CHARADES

Have you ever played charades? It's a game that's been around for over 400 years! It's for two or more people and it's all about miming and guessing words.

Charades is easy to learn and it's a great way to get to know new friends – especially if shyness holds you back from using your voice. Try practising with your grown-up first.

Here's how to play:

- One player thinks of a word and keeps it a secret from the other player or players.

- They have to act out the word – no talking!

- The other player or players have to keep guessing until they get the right answer.

- Once the secret word has been guessed, you can swap around and play again.

# ACTIVITY: DRAW YOUR BIG VOICE

Shyness can make our voices teeny tiny, and bravery can make them big and confident.

Can you draw your big voice in this speech bubble? You could write your name, or "I AM BRAVE" or some magic words from page 53. You can also decorate it with different colours and patterns.

# ACTIVITY: YAY FOR YOU!

What's brave for you is unique to you. Give yourself a pat on the back by designing badges and trophies for your bravest moments.

# PART 3: IT'S OK TO BE ME

Who you are is just right for you. Believing in yourself is the key to unlocking your bravery.

# YOU ARE NOT ALONE

Everyone feels shy, scared and small some of the time. There's nothing wrong with you, and it's OK to feel that way.

You can have all kinds of feelings. Emotions can't hurt you.

You're already brave if you're reading this book and thinking about doing hard things. Every time you feel shy, it's a sign that you're being brave.

# ACTIVITY: MY STRENGTHS

Can you think of ten of your strengths? Bet there are loads more, but there's only room for ten here! Think about things you're good at, things you feel confident doing and kind things other people say about you. For example: "I'm a great friend", "I have a big imagination".

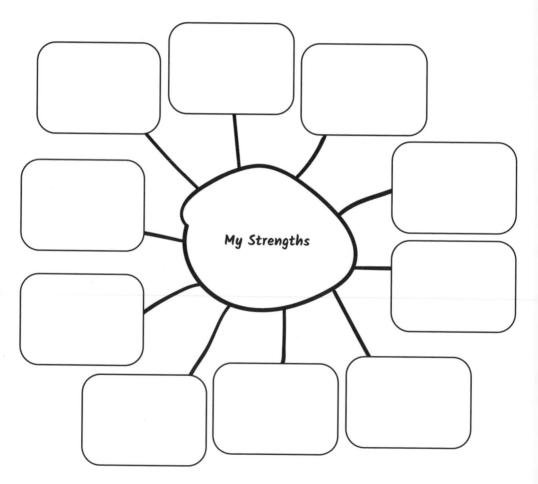

# ACTIVITY: STAND TALL

When Jem feels shy, Jem's body shrinks as small as it can possibly be.

The way we feel has a big effect on how we hold our bodies. But you can flip this around with a clever trick: using your body to change the way you feel.

Try this:
Curl up so you are as small as you can get. How does that feel?

_____

Now, raise your head and straighten your back. Perhaps you're feeling a bit more confident already.

Stand up, making your legs strong and straight. Spread your fingers out like stars and spread your arms out from your body or up to the sky (whichever feels best). Take a deep breath.

How do you feel now?

_____

# ACTIVITY: I LIKE MYSELF

When you like yourself, bravery can grow. Taking some time to draw a picture of yourself gives you a chance to celebrate you. Can you draw a self-portrait on the opposite page? Try looking at yourself in a mirror or a photograph for a guide. You could draw your whole body or just your face – you choose!

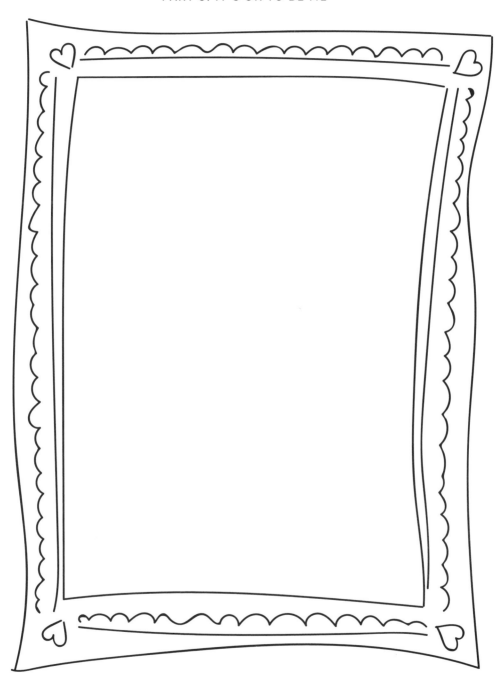

# ACTIVITY: TALK ABOUT YOUR FEELINGS

Your family and good friends want to hear what it's like to be you, so don't be afraid to talk to people you trust about how you feel.

Even if you're worried your feelings don't quite make sense, or if you're not sure how they might make the other person feel, your feelings still matter.

Talking about your feelings is one of the simplest and best ways to feel better and build bravery. Firstly, it helps the other person to get to know the real you. But most importantly, when you say what's on your mind and in your heart to someone you trust, it makes those difficult thoughts, feelings and experiences a little lighter to carry. It's super brave to tell the truth about your emotions.

Draw the people in your life that you feel comfortable talking with about anything? Feelings, random thoughts, problems... Just one person is enough, two or three is plenty, and if you have more, that's great!

# SAYING NO

Saying "no" can sometimes be one of the bravest things in the world. But when you say "no" to something you don't feel comfortable with, don't like or don't have time for, other people can sometimes feel upset.

It's OK for other people to feel difficult feelings. Just like you, other people can feel all feelings.

Sometimes shyness means we don't feel OK with saying "no". It feels scary or even dangerous.

There are lots of ways to say "no". Here are a few to practise. Which ones feel good to say?

No, thank you.

I'd love to, but I can't.

# ACTIVITY: HAVING FUN TOGETHER WHEN IT'S HARD TO TALK

Talking can be super hard, especially to people you don't know very well. Quite often, you can get to know each other better – and have more fun – when you play a game together instead.

Try these games out with a new friend.

## Squares

Pick a different colour pencil each. Take turns to draw a line between two dots. The aim of the game is for your coloured lines to complete a square. You can stop the other player from making a square by using your colour to draw a line there first. When you complete a square, put the first letter of your name in the middle. When all the dots are joined up the winner is the player with the most squares.

# Mirror me

One person is the leader and the other person must follow them. The leader draws a shape on one side of the line and the follower has to draw it as if the line were a mirror. Swap round after 60 seconds and keep swapping until the page is filled with mirrored drawings. There's no winner or loser in this game!

Don't worry if you don't have this book with you – all you need is a piece of paper and a pencil each!

# DON'T COMPARE YOURSELF TO OTHERS

Have you ever heard the saying "comparison is the thief of joy" and wondered what it means?

When we compare ourselves to other people, life becomes a competition. When someone is taller than you, comparison makes you think you're too short, or vice versa. When life is a competition, it's very hard to be happy. We are either losing and feeling bad about ourselves or winning and thinking badly of others. That's why comparing ourselves to others steals the joy from life.

Do you compare yourself to other people? It might be celebrities, friends or family… even strangers you see out and about. It's very normal to compare yourself to others.

> Remember, when you compare yourself, you might decide you're better than the other person or worse. Both are comparison and both steal happiness!

What parts of yourself do you compare? Circle any of these and add your own if you think of more…

The way
you look

Your
hobbies

The things
you have

Your parents
or carers

Your school
work

# When you feel jealous

Sometimes you might feel jealous when you think someone else has more than you or is cleverer or better looking. This might lead you to feel shy about your intelligence or the way you look. Jealousy is a really hard emotion. If you're feeling jealousy, it's OK. Try writing all your jealous thoughts in a journal.

A good way to turn jealous feelings into calm ones is to use gratitude. Can you think of three things you're grateful for in your life?

| 1 | 2 | 3 |
|---|---|---|

# When you feel like you're better than others

The other side of comparison is when you decide you are the winner of the comparison competition. If you think this, it's OK. It can feel good to think this way, and it's important to celebrate yourself when you've done a good job. But if you can only feel good by thinking other people aren't as good as you, you don't really believe in yourself.

A good way to transform this is to build your empathy skills, or your sense of how others are feeling.. Think of the person you compared yourself to. If they knew about the comparison competition, how do you think they would feel about it?

Then ask yourself: how would you feel if they'd decided you were the loser?

# BUILD EMPATHY TO BEAT COMPARISON

Whether you usually decide you are the winner or the loser of your comparison competition, empathy can help.

Empathy means imagining how another person feels, why they might act the way they do or have the kind of life they have. Having empathy for others also helps you to be kind to yourself, because it's about understanding that everyone is different, no one is perfect and we are all trying our best.

When we grow our empathy skills, other people become less scary, because we learn that we are all a bit scared, unsure and shy.

Think about these emotions – have you felt any of them today? Then take a look at the bubbles on the next page and see which emotions could go with which bubble.

| | |
|---|---|
| Sad | Surprised |
| Jealous | Bored |
| Angry | Lonely |
| Excited | Guilty |
| Calm | Grateful |
| Worried | Disappointed |
| Shy | Embarrassed |
| Panic | Happy |

If these things happened to you, how would you feel? Write one or more emotions in each bubble.

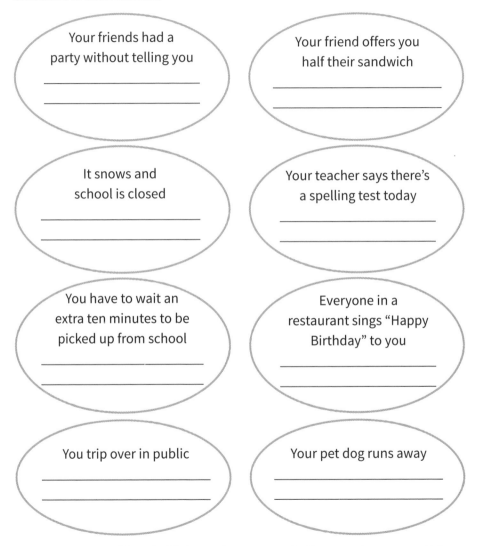

Your friends had a party without telling you

_____

_____

Your friend offers you half their sandwich

_____

_____

It snows and school is closed

_____

_____

Your teacher says there's a spelling test today

_____

_____

You have to wait an extra ten minutes to be picked up from school

_____

_____

Everyone in a restaurant sings "Happy Birthday" to you

_____

_____

You trip over in public

_____

_____

Your pet dog runs away

_____

_____

Other people would probably have the same or similar emotions to you if these things happened to them. Or, they might feel differently, and that's OK, too.

# ACTIVITY: MY BRAVE HOUSE

You are brilliant exactly as you are. Can you decorate this house to show some of the parts of your life?

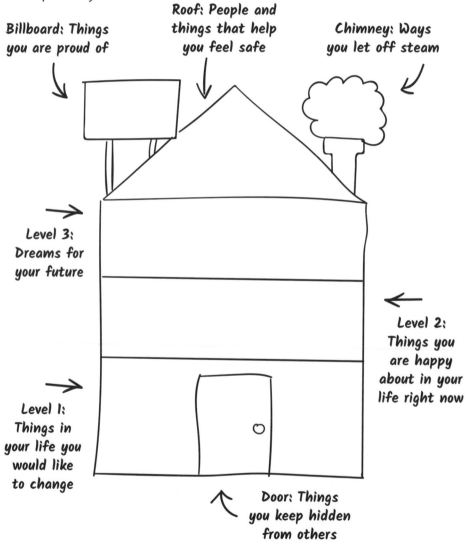

**Billboard: Things you are proud of**

**Roof: People and things that help you feel safe**

**Chimney: Ways you let off steam**

**Level 3: Dreams for your future**

**Level 2: Things you are happy about in your life right now**

**Level 1: Things in your life you would like to change**

**Door: Things you keep hidden from others**

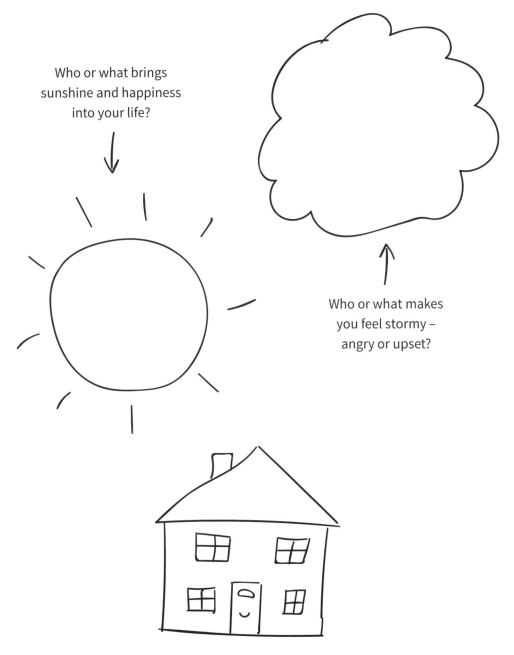

Who or what brings
sunshine and happiness
into your life?

Who or what makes
you feel stormy –
angry or upset?

# I AM
# A GOOD
# FRIEND

# PERFECT DOESN'T EXIST

A lot of the people and characters you see on TV, the internet and in magazines might look perfect to you. It can affect how you feel about yourself if you don't look, think or behave like they do.

Did you know special lights and computer tricks are used to make them look the way they do? Famous people are normal human beings, just like you. The only difference is that they use special lights and computer tricks so they can look a certain way when lots of people will see them.

Perfect doesn't actually exist. We all have different ideas about what looks good, what music sounds good and what's interesting. The best kinds of people are those who understand that their own favourites are probably not everybody else's favourites, and that's OK.

If someone tries to make you feel bad because of how you look, it's not your body, face, clothes or hair that needs to change, it's their attitude.

You are unique, and there's no need to change yourself to be more like someone else.

# ACTIVITY: FEED YOUR MIND GOOD THINGS

Our minds are really hungry, always gobbling up the things we see and hear. Our minds make sense of the things we feed them, and this affects how we feel about ourselves, other people and the world around us. So, it's important to make smart choices about the things you feed your hungry mind.

Have you ever thought about the kinds of people you see on TV or the internet and read about in books or magazines?

What are your favourite books, films and TV shows?

Can you write down some of your favourite characters? What do you like about them?

If you want to build bravery, feed your mind characters who are like you as well as characters who are different to you. Try to think of some of your favourite characters who…

**Make mistakes**

**Solve problems**

**Have lots of emotions**

**Are brave**

**Have fun**

**Stand up for themselves**

**Work together**

# ACTIVITY: MY FEAR SAYS, MY BRAVERY SAYS...

We all have different voices inside us telling us different things. Some of the voices are louder than others. Some are kind and some are mean. Some are scared and some are brave.

Think of something that makes you feel small, scared or shy. Draw or write it here:

What does your scared, fearful voice inside say about it?

Now, can you hear your brave voice? Listen carefully. What does that voice have to say?

# PART 4: HOW TO BE BRAVE

In this chapter you'll discover the secret to finding bravery in any situation.

# ACTIVITY: MY BRAVERY SHRINKERS

What are the things that bring feelings of shyness into your mind and body? Perhaps they make you want to shrink so you're tiny, curl up into a ball, run away or disappear in a puff of smoke.

It could be a type of place – like somewhere that's really loud or busy. It could be something someone else says or does – like whispering or leaving you out. Or it could be a particular situation – like school or birthday parties.

Write a list of things that shrink your bravery here:

_____

_____

_____

_____

_____

_____

_____

In the next chapter we're going to learn about how to be brave, even when one of these things is happening.

# ACTIVITY: MAKE A PLAN

Now you have a list of your bravery shrinkers, you have the chance to grow your bravery so it's less of a problem. Let's investigate.

Choose just one of your bravery shrinkers to think about – write it here:

_____

_____

_____

How do you feel when you think about this situation? Circle any that sound right to you:

| | | | |
|---|---|---|---|
| Embarrassed | Scared | Anxious | Like running away |
| Like hiding | Angry | Tired | Frozen to the spot |

Add your own:

_____

_____

_____

How does it feel in your body? You can use words, patterns, colours and symbols – whichever works best for you.

What does your inner voice tell you about the situation? For example…
"I'll be laughed at."
"I'll be left out."
"No one likes me."
"I won't be able to speak."
"Everyone will be better at it than me."

Building bravery is hard work, and you're doing great. You might like to use the activity on page 48 to tell a kinder story to yourself, or practise your power words from page 46/47 before you move on to the next part.

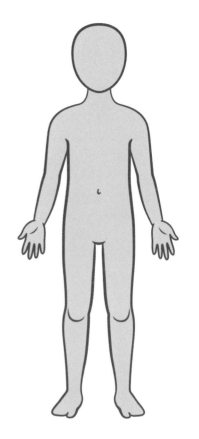

## Steps toward bravery

The best way to build bravery is to take small steps toward your goal. When Jem thinks about speaking up in class, Jem's mind fills with worries.

How can Jem break it down into small steps?

On the next pages you'll learn how to break any goal down into steps that work for you.

# TOOL 1: ALL FEELINGS ARE NORMAL

Everyone feels emotions all day long – even if they don't show it on the outside. Most people don't show every emotion they have on the outside, so when you're feeling a difficult emotion it can seem like you're the only one.

So, if you're feeling shy, that's OK!
If you're feeling anxious, that's OK!
If you're feeling angry, that's OK!

All feelings are OK feelings, and none of them can hurt you or stop you from doing hard things.

# ACTIVITY: BE MINDFUL OF FEELINGS

When you're feeling a big emotion – such as anxious, embarrassed or scared – you can use mindfulness to remind yourself that everything is OK.

Here's how:

- Stop what you are doing

- Put your hand on your heart

- Take a deep breath

- Say to yourself – silently or out loud – "I am feeling _____."

- Take another deep breath

- Say to yourself – silently or out loud – "I am safe. It's OK to feel _____."

# TOOL 2: MAKE A COMIC STRIP

You can make a comic strip as a way of practising bravery with drawing, writing and your imagination.

Jem's goal is to speak up in class next time Jem knows the answer to a question.

Now you try! Make your own comic strip using this template:

# TOOL 3: PRACTISE, PRACTISE, PRACTISE

Getting yourself more used to the feelings and situations you find difficult will help you to be brave. You can add lots of practice steps to your bravery plan. Here are a few to choose from:

 Walk or drive past the place

 Role-play alone

 Role-play with friends

 Role-play with family

 Role-play with toys

 Make up a song or poem about how you're going to be brave

 Design a game where you make brave choices in order to win

The more your mind gets used to the idea of being brave in tricky situations, the better you'll cope when you're there in real life!

I CAN
TAKE IT
ONE STEP
AT A TIME

# TOOL 4: TAKE YOUR TIME

Doing things at your own pace is one of the keys to building bravery. You get to choose what you do and don't do, and you can break challenges down so they don't feel so big, scary and difficult.

Jem isn't ready to speak up in class yet. That's OK! Jem can get on with the work and know the answers without speaking loudly. Knowing that it's OK to take your time means Jem can relax and concentrate on feeling comfortable in class.

Try not to compare yourself with others and don't put pressure on yourself. Stick with a trusted friend or adult if that helps you feel more comfortable. You're doing great.

Have a think about a challenge you're building bravery for right now. What parts of it feel OK and comfortable? What are you thinking of trying next? What are you not OK with?

What feels OK now…

_____

_____

_____

_____

What I'd like to try next…

_____

_____

_____

_____

What I'm not OK with right now…

_____

_____

_____

_____

# TOOL 5: KNOW YOUR COPING TOOLS

When we feel shy or uncomfortable, everyone has little ways to make themselves feel more comfortable and boost their bravery. These are called "coping tools" and most of us don't know we're using them!

Wiggling fingers makes Jem feel calmer and braver.

Do you use any of these coping tools? Circle any that you do.

*Putting your hands in your pockets*      *Folding your arms*      *Biting your nails*      *Picking at your skin or clothes*

*Talking about your feelings*      *Playing with your hair*      *Taking a deep breath*      *Putting your hood up*

*Looking at the ground*      *Not talking*      *Bouncing your feet*

It's OK to use tools to help you feel braver and more comfortable (as long as you're not hurting yourself or others). Some of the tools on the list can actually make things worse for you. Anything that stops you being yourself (like not talking), hurts your body (like nail-biting) or damages your clothing might help you feel more comfortable in the moment, but it will actually shrink bravery in the long run. Can you use a different colour to colour in the bravery-shrinking coping tools on the list?

# PICK-AND-MIX HEALTHY COPING TOOLS

Did you spot any bravery-shrinking coping tools that you use? It's OK if you did, and you haven't done anything wrong.

Now that you know about bravery-shrinking coping tools, you can experiment swapping them with bravery-building coping tools instead.

Here are some more bravery-building coping tools. Which will you try?

 Saying your power words

 Naming your emotions

 Asking for help

 Sticking close to a buddy

 54321 senses

 Squeezing a stress toy

 Playing with putty

 Breathing exercises

# ACTIVITY: DRAW YOUR STEPS

Now you have loads of tools for your bravery steps! Here are Jem's bravery steps:

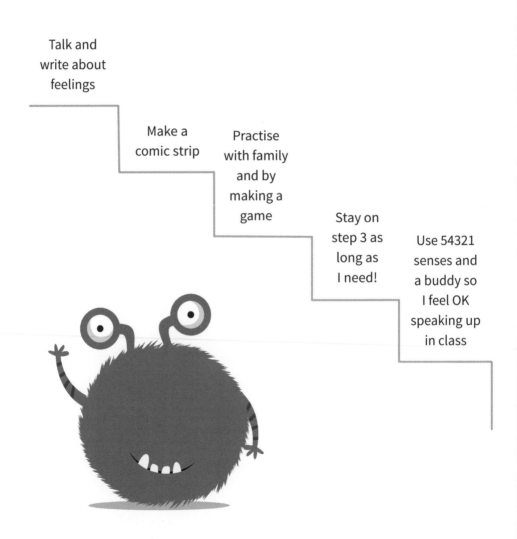

Talk and write about feelings

Make a comic strip

Practise with family and by making a game

Stay on step 3 as long as I need!

Use 54321 senses and a buddy so I feel OK speaking up in class

Now you can make your own!

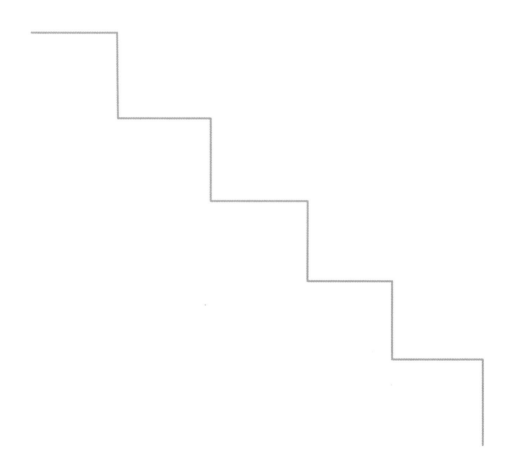

# WHAT IS AVOIDANCE?

"Avoidance" is a word we use for when someone makes an effort not to do something, because that thing feels too scary or risky.

It makes perfect sense to avoid things that feel really scary, right? Of course!

Some things should be avoided because they aren't safe, like deep water or broken glass.

But when we avoid things that only feel frightening but aren't actually dangerous – like making new friends or speaking up in class – we miss out on all sorts of great things.

What's more, the longer we avoid things, the bigger and scarier they become in our minds, and the harder it is to find the bravery to face these fears.

It's OK if there are things you avoid. It takes a lot of bravery to face your fears and it's OK if you're not ready yet.

# HOW YOUR BRAIN LEARNS

Brains love to know exactly what's going to happen in the future. It's a pity that's impossible! Brains try their best anyway and use the things that have happened in the past to try and predict what will happen in the future. Brains use emotions to help them learn.

If you were once laughed at for getting a question wrong in class, that might have made you feel a big, huge emotion like embarrassment. The bigger the emotion, the more important your brain will think it was.

So, even if you got lots of questions correct before (and that made you feel a smaller, positive emotion) your brain will remember the time you felt the huge emotion most of all.

The good news is, your brain is always learning, so if you use your bravery to do hard things and show your brain that everything is OK, it will slowly relax and learn that it's safe to be brave.

If you avoid being brave, your brain will not learn this. Being brave will always feel scary the first few times while your brain gets used to it.

# WHEN PEOPLE ARE BRAVERY SHRINKERS

A lot of people feel shy around others. Maybe you feel comfortable around people you know really well and uncomfortable around new people. You might feel yourself going quiet or embarrassed even when you're with friends. You can beat embarrassment or anxiety by moving your body as if you are brave and confident. Try sitting up tall and taking a really deep breath.

You can beat quietness by asking questions. You don't need to be loud, say lots or come up with unusual ones. Something simple like "What did you do yesterday?" or "Do you have any pets?" will help you feel more comfortable and get a conversation going.

> **Hint:** Try to add a question each time you speak, to keep the conversation going!

Can you add a few more conversation-starting questions? Here are a few to get you started:

What book are you reading at the moment?

If you feel shy, scared or worried around someone in particular because they are unkind to you, hurt you or get you to do things you don't want to do, that's different. You don't have to talk to them or try to feel braver. Talk to a trusted grown-up if this is happening to you.

# I AM
# BRILLIANT
# EXACTLY
# AS I AM

# SPEAKING UP

Being shy can often mean it's hard to ask for help or speak up for yourself when something unfair happens (like someone pushing in front of you) or someone makes an honest mistake (like giving you a type of food you don't like eating). Worrying about how other people will react when you speak up for yourself is a big bravery shrinker. Remember that you can't control other people's emotions or actions. If they are angry or unkind, that doesn't mean you were wrong to speak up.

As long as you make sure you're:

 polite

 truthful

 loud enough to be heard

… you're doing nothing wrong.

# FEELING SHY ABOUT YOUR BODY

Your body belongs to you. Sometimes you might feel shy about how your body looks, something it does or how it moves, and this can stop you from enjoying fun things like swimming, running, dancing or playing sports.

   If that sounds like you, can you write down a few words about your body?

What about your body makes you feel shy?

_____

What kind of words do you use to describe this?

_____

Can you choose some kinder words?

_____

Write down three things you're grateful to your body for (for example, strong lungs, good at climbing, excellent cuddler).

_____

Try to choose your kinder words and focus on all the brilliant things your body is capable of doing, rather than what it looks like.

# I AM ALWAYS LEARNING AND GROWING

# ACTIVITY: FLIP YOUR THOUGHTS

There is always more than one way of thinking about things, and changing how you think changes how brave you feel.

Jem is visiting a friend's house for dinner. It's pizza night, but there's pepperoni on the pizza and Jem is a vegetarian. Jem thinks: Oh no! I'll have to go hungry! Jem is scared to say anything in case Jem's friend thinks Jem is fussy or rude. Jem could keep quiet and miss out on eating, or eat the pepperoni pizza even though it feels wrong. Or, Jem could turn the shy thought into a brave one: They didn't know I don't eat meat. I can tell them now and ask if I could have something else to eat.

The secret to flipping shy thoughts into brave ones is to work out what you are really thinking and feeling. Here's how you do it:

| Shy thought | What I really think | Flip it! |
|---|---|---|
| I must keep quiet. → | I'm worried what people will think of me. → | I can speak up for myself. |
| I'm rubbish at this. → | I tried before and wasn't perfect. → | I can practise and each time I do, it will get easier. |
| I can't do this. → | I'm scared I won't be able to do it. → | I can try my best and ask for help. |

Can you add your own?

| Shy thought | What I really think | Flip it! |
| --- | --- | --- |
| → | | → |
| → | | → |
| → | | → |
| → | | → |
| → | | → |
| → | | → |

# BE YOU

Shyness can sometimes stop you from being yourself – it can make you quieter than you'd like to be, which can mean other people don't get to know the real you.

Sometimes the idea that another person might not like you can stop you from saying what you really think, or how you really feel.

Imagine for a moment that everybody wanted to be your best friend. It might be fun for a while, but it would soon get totally exhausting. The truth is, not everyone is going to be a good fit for you as a friend. Everyone is unique, a bit like a puzzle piece. Each puzzle piece fits nicely with some puzzle pieces but doesn't really fit with others… and that's OK!

If you don't let your real self shine, it's impossible to find who you fit with. As long as you are respectful of others, you can be yourself and find the people you fit with.

# BRAVERY IS FEELING FEAR AND DOING IT ANYWAY

# STORIES OF BRAVERY

## I asked for help

I'm very good at coding, and I usually don't need help with my projects from anyone else. Once I got stuck – there was a bug I couldn't fix. I tried everything I could think of! I felt embarrassed and I didn't want to ask for help. I wanted to turn off the computer and quit coding forever. Instead, I asked Mum for help and we solved the problem together.

**Billy, 8**

## I tried something new

I used to feel quite embarrassed riding my bike, because I thought everyone else was better at it and they might laugh at me. But I really, really, really didn't want to do extra cycling tuition – it sounded embarrassing too! My parents made me do the tuition and it was hard and I hated it. But after that I felt more confident on my bike. I'm proud of my cycling now.

**Ella, 10**

## I was honest about my feelings

When my parents split up my world changed a lot. I really missed living with both of them but I was worried that speaking about my feelings would upset them. So, I wrote my parents a letter each about how I was feeling. They were both really kind and listened to me when I was ready to talk about it. I feel much more comfortable talking about my feelings now: both my parents love me and my feelings matter.

**Frida, 9**

## I faced my fears

When I was younger, I was scared of horses. I felt so shy I didn't even want to look at them! My carer took me to a stables and for the first session I just spent time with the horses while they were tied up. Then over time I learned how to groom the horses, how to pick out their feet, lead them, until one day I wanted to try riding. My carer and the staff at the stables let me go at my own pace. Now I go riding often, and I feel really comfortable and confident.

**Rafferty, 11**

## I stood up to bullies

My best friend has dyslexia, which makes some school work hard for him. Some other children were making fun of him in the playground. I felt really scared and I wanted to run away, even though they weren't talking to me. But instead I used the biggest voice I could to tell the bullies to stop it. I put my arm around my best friend and we went to find a grown-up who could help us.

**Omar, 7**

## I shared my creativity

I love painting. I paint lots in my room using 3D paint and little canvasses. No one used to get to see my paintings, though, in case they thought they were stupid. At school we did a painting project and our work got displayed in the main hall. It felt good for other people to see something I'd painted. I felt proud of my work. Now I feel braver about other people seeing my paintings at home. My family really like receiving my paintings as birthday presents.

**Abbie, 10**

# PART 5: TAKING GOOD CARE OF YOURSELF

Looking after your body and mind will help you become your best and bravest self.

# TIME TO CHILL

Taking time to relax is really important; it helps keep your mind and body strong and healthy. Why not try one of these relaxing activities:

- Go for a bike ride
- Paint a picture
- Write a story or poem
- Play a card game
- Do some stretches
- Make beaded jewellery
- Do some baking with an adult
- Learn to weave, knit or crochet

# ACTIVITY: MAKE YOUR OWN RELAXATION PUTTY BALLS

Use this simple recipe to make your own super-satisfying squeezy putty ball to help you relax.

You will need:

 1 grown-up to help you

 1 cup hair conditioner

 2 cups cornflour/cornstarch

 5 uninflated balloons

Combine the conditioner and the cornflour in a large mixing bowl.

Knead the mixture to form a smooth dough.

Stretch the balloon open and poke a little bit of dough in at a time. You can blow some air in to help the dough settle into a ball at the bottom.

Keep adding dough until the balloon is filled with enough to make a palm-sized ball.

Make sure there's no air left in the balloon, then tie it up. Your relaxation ball is ready to be squidged!

> **You can stretch another balloon over your putty ball to make it extra durable.**

# KEEPING SAFE ON THE INTERNET

The internet can be a brilliant place! There are so many interesting, inspiring and fun things to learn, and the internet can help you find them. But it's really important to stick to the rules of internet safety when you're online.

Remember:

☺ Never post your personal information or passwords online

☺ Never befriend someone on the internet if you don't know them in real life

☺ Never meet up with someone you met online

☺ Think carefully before you post pictures or words on the internet

☺ If you see something online that makes you feel uncomfortable, unsafe or worried, leave the website, turn off your computer and tell a trusted grown-up straight away

If someone online or in real life asks you to break any of these rules, tell a trusted grown-up.

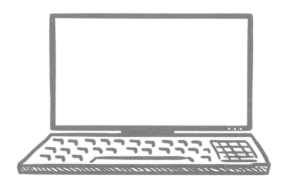

# GETTING PLENTY OF SLEEP

When you sleep, your mind and body can rest, grow and get ready for a new day. If you have trouble getting to sleep, try this trick:

 Get cosy and lie in your bed with no distractions

 Listen to your breathing

 Take a deep breath in to the count of three, then out to the count of three

 Now make your breaths longer – breathe in for four, and out for four

 Keep counting your breaths in and out, until you fall asleep

Having a good night's sleep means you will feel happier, more relaxed and more confident the next day.

# ACTIVITY: TIME TO PLAY

One of the best ways to relax, learn and have fun all at once is by playing. Playing isn't just for little kids. The ways we play might change as we get older, but it's still very important – even for grown-ups!

If you get stuck for things to play, you could make a special dice with some ideas to help you decide.

You will need:

 A dice

 Plain white stickers

 Pen or pencil

Cut the stickers so they are the right size to fit one on each face of the dice.

On each sticker, write one of your favourite things to play.

Stick a sticker on each face of the dice.

Throw the dice whenever you feel bored or can't decide what to play.

Here are some ideas for your dice:

Do a jigsaw

Construction toys

Teddies or dolls

Junk modelling

Colouring

Dressing up

# MY BODY
# IS PRECIOUS

# EAT HEALTHILY

When you eat a balanced diet and drink plenty of water, your body will feel good, and so will your mind!

What does your body need to be healthy?

Carbohydrates like bread and pasta to give you energy.

Proteins like eggs, beans and fish to help repair itself.

Fats like butter, cheese and oils to store energy for later.

Fibre-rich foods like fruits and vegetables to help digestion.

Water to help fight off diseases, keep you cool and digest your food.

Plus a few treats now and then for energy and enjoyment.

# ACTIVITY: DESIGN A HEALTHY MEAL

Using the facts about healthy eating from the last page, can you use this page to draw a healthy, delicious meal that you'd love to eat?

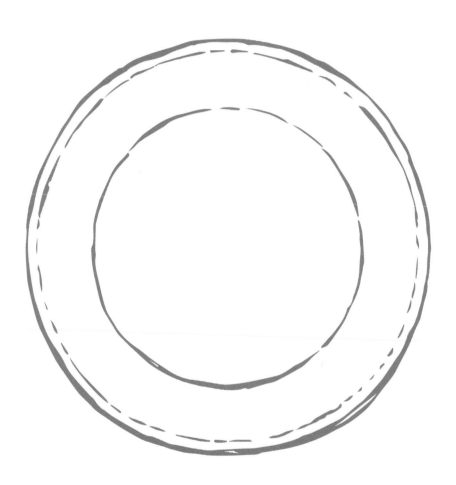

# EXCELLENT EXERCISE

Exercise is really important for keeping your body healthy, but did you know it's also really good for your mind?

Here are just some of the reasons why:

Reaching a goal like swimming 50 metres gives a feeling of accomplishment

Practising a skill like table tennis builds self-esteem and confidence

Getting out of breath helps you feel relaxed and calm

Playing or practising with others helps you make new friends

# ACTIVITY: DANCE YOUR WORDS

Dancing is a great way to increase your confidence, get rid of anxious feelings and have fun.

Here's a funny dancing game you can play with family or friends!

Set a timer for one minute. Put some music on and think of a word to spell using your body. Move in time with the music, turning your body into one letter at a time. The other players have to guess the word before the timer runs out.

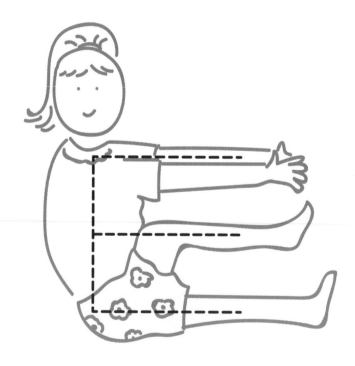

# I AM KIND
## TO MYSELF

# ACTIVITY: YOUR SPACE

Your bedroom is an important place. It's where you wind down from the day and sleep. It's easier to be brave when you've had enough sleep.

Can you draw your bedroom here?

Do you ever find it hard to get to sleep? What thoughts or feelings make it difficult for you?

_____

_____

_____

_____

Here are some ideas to try – they might make falling asleep a little bit easier for you.

- A cosy blanket
- Talking to and cuddling up with your grown-up at bedtime
- Writing your thoughts and feelings in a journal
- Having a warm bath
- Making sure you have the same bed-time routine every evening
- Reading a book

# UNPLUG YOURSELF

Using a computer, tablet, phone or watching TV is fun, and there are loads of interesting and useful things the internet can help us with.

But screen time can also make us feel more anxious, more shy and more negative about ourselves – in other words, it can be a bravery shrinker! That's why it's important to balance screen time with time away from screens.

What do you like to do when it's not screen time?

_____

_____

_____

_____

Have you thought of trying out these ideas?

**Build a fort**

**Make origami**

**Write a story**

**Go outside**

**Write a poem**

**Paint your nails**

Rearrange
your
bedroom

Write
a letter

Try out a
new recipe

Make a time
capsule

Write your
life story

Learn a
card trick

Read a
magazine

Learn to
play chess

Make slime

Design a
treasure
hunt

Bounce on a
trampoline

# PART 6: CELEBRATE YOURSELF

You've nearly finished the book! Time to recap and think about how you can use what you've learned to build and spread bravery.

I am great!

# ACTIVITY: WHAT I'VE LEARNED

You've reached the final part of the book! You superstar! Let's recap what you've learned.

There is strength in shyness.
What do you love most about being you?

_____

You are brilliant exactly as you are.
What's one brilliant thing about you?

_____

There are ways to build bravery that work well for you.
What builds your bravery?

_____

You can do hard things.
What hard thing will you do next?

_____

The more you take good care of yourself, the braver you can be.
How do you take care of yourself?

_____

# ACTIVITY: MAKE AN ACTION PLAN

In the book we've thought a lot about how it feels when shyness takes over and bravery is really hard to find. There have been lots of ideas. Which ones work best for you? Let's make an action plan to help you feel calm, safe and brave.

When I feel…

_____

I can talk to…

_____

I can write, say or think power words like…

_____

I can move my body to feel better by doing…

_____

I can say to others…

_____

# ACTIVITY: KEEP A JOURNAL

You've nearly made it to the end of this book, but that doesn't mean you have to stop thinking and writing about yourself and your experiences.

Why not start a journal using a diary or notebook? A good tip for starting out is to write every evening before you go to bed. Think of one thing from the day that was OK, one tricky thing and one thing that was good.

Try it here!

One thing that was good today…

_____

One thing that was tricky today…

_____

One thing that was OK today…

_____

# ACTIVITY: SPREAD THE BRAVERY!

Now that you've learned so much about bravery, why not make a poster to help other children feel brave enough to be themselves and do hard things?

First, think about what your poster will say, or what the picture will show. Perhaps it could be something you learned in this book that you didn't realize before, or some words that help you feel brave.

You could use drawing, painting, photos, pictures from a magazine, collage or cool lettering.

Sketch some ideas here:

**There's space on the next page for designing your poster neatly!** ⟶

# PART 6: CELEBRATE YOURSELF

Be careful when cutting out your poster! Where will you stick it up?

# MY
# FEELINGS
# MATTER

# THE END

Jem knows all about how to build bravery now. Do you?

You can come back to this book any time you like – whether it's to boost your own bravery or help a friend understand bravery a bit better. You've worked really hard and should be very proud of yourself.

Don't forget: it's OK to be you, and you can be brave any time!

# I AM
# BRAVE

# For parents: What you can do to help boost your child's bravery

Real bravery looks different to how it is portrayed in books and movies. In real life, being brave can mean saying "no" to something you feel obliged to do but really don't want to… or saying "yes" to something that might inconvenience others. It can mean speaking up in a work meeting or saying "sorry" when we mess up. The same goes for children: the bravest child in the class is often the one who comes last in a race or the one whose voice shakes when they speak.

The single best way you can help your child build bravery is by being patient with them. It might feel tempting to dismiss feelings of shyness and anxiety and encourage your child to go "in at the deep end", but the sad truth is, while this may change their behaviour in the short term, it doesn't get to the root of what's going on emotionally for them.

When children feel understood by the adults around them, they feel more able to strike out on their own, use their voice and be brave. Let your child know that they can take their time and that you are there for them for as long as they need you to be. When a child hears this, it helps them relax, take the pressure off themselves and push themselves in ways that feel comfortable, because they know that you will be kind and understanding, even if things go wrong.

By being a kind, empathetic listener, you will help your child grow emotionally strong and resilient. As your child grows, they will be secure in the knowledge that you are on their team and there for them no matter what.

I do hope this book has been helpful for you and your child. It's so hard to see them missing out or shrinking themselves out of shyness, and you're doing a great job by acknowledging their feelings and guiding them toward ways to build up their bravery and self-assurance.

Wishing you all the very best of luck – your child is lucky to have you on their team!

# Further advice

If you're worried about your child's mental health, do talk it through with your GP. While almost all children experience feelings of shyness, some may need extra help. There are lots of great resources out there for information and guidance on children's mental health. Here are just a few:

**Mind (UK)**
www.mind.org.uk
0300 123 3393
info@mind.org.uk
Text: 86463

**BBC Bitesize (UK)**
www.bbc.co.uk/bitesize/support

**Childline (UK)**
www.childline.org.uk
0800 1111

**Child Mind Institute (USA)**
www.childmind.org
(212) 308-3118

**The Youth Mental Health Project (USA)**
www.ymhproject.org
info@ymhproject.org

# Recommended reading

## For children:
*What to Do When You Feel Too Shy* by Claire A. B. Freeland and Jacqueline B. Toner
Magination Press, 2016

*Social Skills Activities for Kids* by Natasha Daniels
Rockridge Press, 2019

*Happy, Healthy Minds* by The School of Life
The School of Life Press, 2020

## For adults:
*Daring Greatly* by Brené Brown
Penguin, 2015

*The Book You Wish Your Parents Had Read* by Philippa Perry
Penguin, 2019

# Image credits

# THE WORRY WORKBOOK
The Worry Warriors' Activity Book

Imogen Harrison

£10.99

Paperback

ISBN: 978-1-78783-537-5

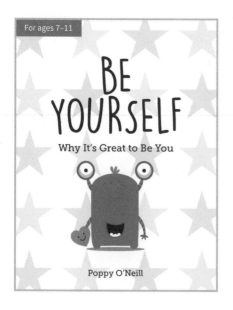

# BE YOURSELF
Why It's Great to Be You

Poppy O'Neill

£10.99

Paperback

ISBN: 978-1-78783-608-2

# DON'T WORRY, BE HAPPY

A Guide to Overcoming Anxiety

Poppy O'Neill

£10.99

Paperback

ISBN: 978-1-78685-236-6

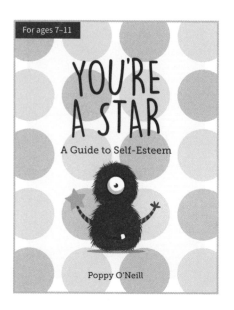

# YOU'RE A STAR

A Guide to Self-Esteem

Poppy O'Neill

£10.99

Paperback

ISBN: 978-1-78685-235-9

If you're interested in finding out more about our books,
find us on Facebook at **Summersdale Publishers**
and follow us on Twitter at **@Summersdale** and
on Instagram at **@SummersdalePublishers**.

**www.summersdale.com**